T0366042

CHANGEARTIST

SURVIVING CHANGE

By JoNel Mundt, Ph. D.
Illustrations by Sandy Gullikson

DEDICATION

This book is dedicated to the many people who helped me through changes, to the memories of the many who influenced me, and to the inspiration of the great artist for this book, Sandy Gullikson.

Sandy, I regret that we did not meet personally. Thank you for believing in this project. This book is dedicated to you, and to your changes.

Copyright © 2003 by JoNel Mundt, PhD. 535053

All rights reserved. No part of this book may
be reproduced or transmitted in any form or by
any means, electronic or mechanical, including
photocopying, recording, or by any information storage
and retrieval system, without permission in writing from
the copyright owner.

To order additional copies of this book, contact:
Xlibris
844-714-8691
www.Xlibris.com
Orders@Xlibris.com

Book Designer: Diana Seciu

ISBN: Softcover   978-1-4134-1446-2

Print information available on the last page

Rev. date: 06/21/2023

THE GREAT DILEMMA—ONE COYOTE'S VIEW

Who am I? Why am I here? Where did I come from? Where am I going? Will I be there by next week?

CONTENTS

Preface

This book was initially written a few years ago. At that time, I had endured many life changes and was seeing the light at the end of the tunnel. Then life took several more large turns. Five years later, I am taking the time to share the many lessons I have learned along the way.

These inflection points or change points require us to view life differently, to respond to life differently, or to live life differently. I learned that there is no steady state— change is continual. Or, perhaps change *is* the steady state.

Through these many changes, I learned a great deal about coping, sometimes gracefully and sometimes less than gracefully. Yet, I live and endure and have transformed much of my life in very positive ways in response to changes that could have undermined me.

In this book, I do not detail my own life. Rather, I offer you, the reader, some of the techniques I use in managing or coping with large and small changes in my world. These have been my survival techniques, and will serve as my reference, reminder, and guide for managing future changes. I write this as much for me as for you, in hopes that it can do the same for you.

Interestingly, many of these techniques are utilized in business (in which I am a professor and consultant), in creativity teachings, and in self-development or personal growth literature.

The book is illustrated by Sandy Gullikson. Many years ago, I purchased Sandy's greeting cards. Wanting more cards and not being able to find them, I phoned the "800-number" on the back of the card. A few minutes later, Sandy returned my call. She told me she liked to get to know her customers, and offered to send me a catalog. She lived in Vermont at the time.

It was a serendipitous encounter. After seeing more of her illustrations, with their whimsical, happy animals combined with their very insightful captions, I realized that Sandy was really speaking about the process of life itself. She seemed to have a soulful, spiritual view of life, combined with wonderful humor. Her inspirational, uplifting designs reminded me very much of the process of change. I always smiled at Coyote and his red cowboy boots.

Sandy and I spoke again, more than once, and I asked if she would be favorable to using her illustrations in this book on change. I sent her the manuscript as it was then, and she was pleased to be part of the project. She said she found it "inspirational and uplifting."

Much of the rest is history, and here is the book that results from the collaboration of Sandy's art and my writing. Sadly, I never met Sandy, who died in 2002 from Lou Gehrig's disease. I hope this book will serve as a commemoration of the inspiration she gave to me and to others through her art. My hope also is that this "Survival Guide" helps you not just cope with changes, but use them as vehicles for growth.

  —JoNel

INTRODUCTION

Why do we care about change, and how we respond to it? Because

. . . change is everywhere. . .

Sure, sometimes we go years in the same groove, but then suddenly something changes in our environment. Our career changes, someone dies, we graduate from college — there are myriad situations that create change. Yes, sometimes it is more obvious than others; sometimes more debilitating than others; sometimes more exhilarating than others. But, it surely seems to be a part of many people's lives.

I observed this primarily from two sources. First, my own life went through several major changes or shifts, whatever we want to call them. *Loss* is the oft-used term. I had most of the changes that are considered major — career changes, relationship changes, financial changes, geographical changes, deaths of friends, my own loss of health. . .

Second, in the mid-nineties, I had interviewed women about what they expected from life, what they got, how they felt about the difference, how they coped, what helped them "keep on keeping on." The book, which is still in process, is called The Ecology of Women's Lives: Expectations, Crossroads, and Outcomes (working title). "Ecology" is the study of relationships between organisms and their environments.

After my own issues derailed the book, I looked up from my myopia to see that the interviews I had made were in some sense outdated. These women's lives had totally *changed* over the course of a few years. I realized that my interviews were but snapshots of moments in time in women's lives.

The interviews themselves were fascinating for me, but the light bulb that went on as a result of those interviews was almost more astounding:

. . .life is a <u>process</u>, even though comprised of moments in time. . .

And so, I am writing about *change* before I return to <u>Ecology.</u>

UNDERSTANDING "CHANGE"

First, it is helpful to understand what is happening in our lives. Change is defined as:

> **Change** (chanj) *v.* **changed, changing, changes.** *–tr.* **1.a.** To cause to be different; alter. *n.* **1.a.** The act, process or result of changing; alternation or modification. **2.** A transition from one state, condition, or phase to another.

Notice that here we are discussing both nouns and verbs. Change may *happen to us* or *we may change.*

I think of change as "cause"—something we must react to. Change in this sense means something in our environment that is altered, requiring us to respond in some way. Change happens around us in our family, our home, our job, our friendships, or our other relationships. It looks something like this:

Environments >>change>>SELF<<change<<Environments

Our responses generally are: resist; do nothing; shift; transition; or transform ourselves. Change can be scary, after all!

At other times, we make *internal shifts*. Perhaps our health changes or perhaps our frame of mind or viewpoints shift for no apparent reason. I call these internal shifts "LifeShifts." Sometimes it is these internal shifts that cause us to change what is happening around us. Our internal changes may make us want to quit our job, or move to the country, for example. It looks something like this:

Environment<< shift<<SELF>>shift>> Environments

Which came first — the chicken or the egg? Did external forces change, hence causing *us* to change? Or did we change internally, thereby creating disruption in our environment? Some people will argue that we attract what we are; if things around us change, really it is *we* that are changing. They argue that our worlds are merely reflections of our own energies.

This book is not designed to sort that out, but rather to say "This is our reality, now how do we determine our future?"

Before I describe some of my own coping strategies, I will say a tiny bit more about catalysts of change and the shapes of change.

INITIATING CHANGE

. . .Everyone has change at some point in life. . .

What are some of the initiators of or catalysts for change — occurrences that set change in motion? I sometimes call these "change drivers": success, loss, failure, lifeshifts, and defining moments.

SUCCESS

We may think we want success, but even the most successful people must cope with changes in their lives that stem from their success. A variety of issues plague successful people; examples include a busier schedule, more stress, escalating power politics, loss of privacy, or conflict between family and work.

LOSS

The necessary coping is very apparent for those subjected to negative change or loss. Examples include loss of a spouse or family member, a career, a self-identity, financial security, or being needed. Even the attainment of a goal, such as earning a degree, can feel like a loss - a loss of that goal, of that process, of the life that accompanied that process, and of the self-identity that goes with the role of student. It seems we lose many things over life, and at times those losses seem overwhelming.

FAILURE

We may feel we fail at attaining certain goals, which causes us embarrassment and loss of self- or social-image. Failure-related terms have negative connotations. Replacing them with a more positive "spin" may be helpful. What seems like failure in any given situation may really be an opportunity for growth, for renewal, or for learning.

LIFESHIFTS

Then there are those whose changes cannot be described as either negative or positive. Some people's personalities, or ways of being, just shift. They must cope, as must others in their world.

Let's use the term "mid-life crisis" as an example. I prefer to use a more positive perspective and call it a "strategic re-evaluation." At certain points in life, we may re-evaluate our situations; where we intended to be in life, and how we are proceeding toward our goals using our current strategies. If those strategies no longer seem workable (meaning, we are not where we want to be, nor will we get there doing what we are doing), we may make a change.

Sometimes external forces keep us from making a change - a partner will not agree, a sick parent must be cared for, etc. In those cases, we desire to make a change but cannot. Regardless, we still need to cope with our shifting perspective.

DEFINING MOMENTS

During life, we have what may be called "defining moments," or moments of significant external change or internal shifts. Perhaps we reach a certain age. Perhaps we find God, or become enlightened. Perhaps, perhaps, perhaps. . .

Regardless, a defining moment may lead to an inner journey or evolutionary process, and we may emerge from that process a transformed individual.

STRUCTURING CHANGE

Our overall responses to change include actively resisting change,   trying to do nothing, shifting, transitioning, and transforming. Notice how these range from resisting change to really adapting to change, and then adopting that change. In the midst of this, we may "plateau" - reach a steady state, a time to catch our breath. We may also end one life before beginning another, and in between we may experience a "wilderness."

The terms below are my own definitions but some people do not differentiate between a change (something that occurs *to* us) and a transition or transformation (something that occurs *within* us). Regardless of how you view these words, imagine you are walking, and imagine what happens to your path and direction in each of the following shapes of change.

You will notice that terms in the preceding section may be thought of as "shapes of change." An inflection point or defining moment suggests that we were on a path, had a major change, and then adjusted our course accordingly. It is this process that makes discussing change so complex. It is helpful to think of life as a journey and we are on a path. What we discuss here relates to that journey and that path.

RESISTING

Most of us resist change, whether the change is for the better or worse. For whatever reason, many of us find change frightening.

DOING NOTHING

In reality, this is not an option. If our environment changes, we are *forced* to accommodate, because we do not live in a vacuum. The alternative - to maintain a steady state - would require us to change to maintain the illusion of non-change.

SHIFTING

Shifting can be thought of as a little change in direction. We were going this way and now we are going in a little different direction - maybe twenty degrees difference.

> **Shift** (shift) *v.* **1.** To move or transfer from one place or position to another. *n.* **2.** A change of direction or form.

TRANSITIONING

Transitioning can be thought of as turning a corner, or making a major internal shift to accommodate the change that is impacting us.

> **Transition** (tran-zish'en, -sish'en) *n.* **1.** The process or an instance of changing from one form, state, activity, or place to another.

TRANSFORMING

I tend to think of transformation as going beyond transition - really "trans*form*ing" from one state to another, or changing form.

> **Transform** (trans-form') *v.* **–formed, -forming, -forms.** *–tr.* **1.** To change markedly the form or appearance of. **2.** To change the nature, function, or condition of; to convert.

> **Transformation** (trans'fer-ma-shen) *n.* **1.a.** The act of transforming. **b.** The state or an instance of being transformed. **c.** Something that has been transformed.

When I think of transformation, I think of a butterfly evolving from a caterpillar. Metamorphosis is growth; mutating is survival.

PLATEAUING

We have seen that we all have change, off and on, during our lifetimes. My own internal shifts were often created through learning and growing. In fact, it sometimes seems as if I go through a growth spurt, then a plateau, followed by then another growth spurt. My observation of faltering partnerships (either business or personal) is that one partner is growing and the other cannot keep up, or that they are growing and plateauing in ways that are not totally coordinated. One partner may seek higher goals, while the other is satisfied with the status quo.

That plateau may be a "wilderness," as described below, or it may merely be a time for us to catch our breaths, to create the external life that coordinates with our new internal reality, or to create a new internal reality that coordinates with our external changes.

ENDINGS, THE WILDERNESS, BEGINNINGS

Some people say that we have to have endings before we have beginnings. Further, between the ending of one way of life and the beginning of another way of life, we are in the wilderness, that place where we feel at odds with our world or that place where we feel confusion without direction. Some people feel so uprooted while they are in the wilderness that they try to turn back and recreate the reality they once had. The notion of endings, the wilderness, and beginnings helps me in remembering that:

- I am not alone in the process of transition: change and transition seem to be the human condition, as well as conditions of nature.

- If I feel directionless, I can understand it by thinking of the wilderness.

- Endings often precede beginnings.

- Without endings, we cannot have beginnings.

Dealing with Today

How do we deal with a new reality in the short-term and in the long-term? Sometimes it can be overwhelming. In this section, I give you a snapshot of many of the ways I found to cope with change. I have kept explanations brief so you can expand on them as you see fit. There is no right or wrong way to cope, but. . .

. . . coping is often the key to survival. . .
and
. . . successful coping may be the key to opportunity. . .

I have drawn on much of my teaching and learning in strategic planning, which is a principle of business that is forward-looking. Here we discuss: observing, creating a sense of place, listening to your Self, staying flexible, visualizing, and indulging your Self.

Step Back, Observe and Ponder
One of the first things we must do is to assess our current situation. We need to collect our thoughts, to think about the changes, and to begin to sort things out toward some level of understanding. We should try to stay nonjudgmental and detached while doing so. We want to make rational decisions for our future.

LISTEN TO AND STUDY SELF

Your Self is that soul you live with. This is a time to really study your Self - to see who it is you have been living with all these years, to see "the stuff you are made of." Exercise your skills in Self-awareness, and learn new ones via reading, conversation and other awareness-building activities. This is discussed in more detail later in this book.

LISTEN TO YOUR ENVIRONMENT

By environment, I mean more than the natural environment - I mean everything that surrounds us, be it our families, our work, our homes, our financial situations, or our neighbors.

This is a time for coping, yes, but also for information-gathering so that you can effectively plan your next move. Open your Self up to the possibilities. Tune in to everything you can and collect information about your current situation and your future opportunities and threats. Although this is discussed in more detail in a later chapter, begin now!

SET THE STAGE: CREATE A SENSE OF PLACE

For this depth of coping, thinking and planning, it is best to have a safe and peaceful place, preferably for both mind and body. Some people meditate, turning their minds into a peaceful place, or read a good book to clear their head. Some people physically move to a more soothing environment - or even a more stimulating one.

PONDER AND CONTEMPLATE

TWO FLOPPED-DOWN BENEVOLENT COYOTES

They whiled away the afternoon contemplating just why grasshoppers are sweeter in June and other mysteries that make up Life's Deepest Meanings.   S Gullikson '85

Alternatively, you can go for a nature walk, go to a museum or dress up your home to create a more soothing or peaceful space. Even fresh flowers give me a sense of peace and place, regardless of the setting.

"Place" has power over us, so we need to tune in to our space and our place, and make it as positive a force as we can. Our investment in surroundings gives us a return-on-investment on the quality of our thinking. Plus, it makes the experience of living more joyful in the process!

STAY FLEXIBLE

During change, it is helpful to stay flexible. The natural tendency is to resist change, but we may not have that choice. Our future direction may be uncertain, and staying flexible seems to help manage the peaks and valleys.

Just as it is important to stay physically limber, it is also important to stay mentally limber—to be able to bend and twist when needed.

BEGIN TO VISUALIZE

It is time to begin trying to visualize a new reality, a new future. Notice what excites you, or stimulates you or gives you a sense of well-being.

LISTEN TO YOUR ENVIRONMENT

Sometimes what Coyote liked to do best was just to STAND QUIETLY in the company of several trees, of different ages and temperaments naturally, and catch up on all of the forest gossip. ©Sandy Gullikson

INDULGE YOUR SELF

Sometimes, indulging our Self can be helpful in maintaining the calm that we need for clear-headedness, or in generating the stimulation that we need to creatively focus on our futures. Cheap thrills and little luxuries can go a long way toward brightening a day or a room, or toward stimulating our minds.

Cheap thrills include the little indulgences that make life feel good. It might be a nice cup of coffee, a good bottle of wine, a flower in a vase, a nice bar of soap, a great coffee mug, a good cup of homemade soup, a delicious chocolate, a movie, a good book, a high quality golf ball, a visit with a friend, or some time for letter-writing.

FINDING THE GOOD STUFF

In this section, we discuss how to make the best of most situations, how to cope in the short-term, and how to make lemonade out of lemons, if that is what life gives us! This includes: looking for the joy, living in abundance, seeking a spiritual outlook, appreciating our oneness, finding your creativity, claiming your goodness, and balancing connection and detachment.

LOOK FOR THE JOY

We can see the world as a very dark place, full of hatred and threats, or we can see it as a positive place, full of energy, love and opportunity. I find that the way I view the world seems to come back to me in the way I am viewed by others. And, having a positive outlook, despite our hardships or successes, makes every day better and brighter for our Self and for others.

There are times, however, when this is so difficult that it becomes impossible. I have had those times. I am not a psychiatric professional, and you should not view me as one. If you are in great anguish, it can be lifesaving to seek the help of a spiritual counselor or of a professional psychiatrist or therapist.

FIND YOUR CREATIVITY

Being creative helps soothe my soul, while at the same time offering me the feeling of being productive, which is a lesson I learned while growing up in a northern European culture. I write and I paint in response to many years of change in my life. My grandfather began painting when he was about seventy years old, in response to retirement.

Earlier in life, I baked cookies or baked bread to relieve stress, or just to gain a sense of calm. Sometimes being creative is a *reflection* of the peace we feel internally.

Being creative does not require you to write a book or paint a picture. It may mean changing something in your home, arranging flowers, creating a card, or sawing a board. It means *creating* - making something different or new:

> **Create** (kre-at') **1.** To cause to exist; bring into being. **2.** To give rise to; produce. **3.** To produce through artistic or imaginative effect.

Begin now to tap into your creativity. It will help you later, in developing options.

CLAIM YOUR GOODNESS: SEEK VALIDATION

It is easy, if we have faced loss or feel we have failed, to think less of ourselves. It is important to claim your goodness among humankind, to look for your strengths, to focus on them, and to validate your own existence through your mental processing. Without that, survival and living can be extremely difficult. Your sense of self-worth and self-esteem is imperative to addressing your future.

LOOK FOR THE JOY

With the rose-colored glasses, Coyote saw that the world was really made of LOVE afterall.

©S. Gulliksn

Live in Abundance

We can live as if there were never enough, or we can live as if there is always enough - enough food, enough money, enough possessions, enough love. Living in abundance is changing your perspective from one of fear to one of love and faith.

Seek a Spiritual Outlook

Nothing is as uplifting as connecting with God, and connecting with our personal spirituality. During the good times, it is tempting to feel invincible. During dark times, it is easy to forget that there is a larger force at work, and we are part of it.

Appreciate our Oneness

It is easy to forget that we are all part of the same godliness in this Universe. We are here to love and serve one another - not torment or criticize or make life difficult for one another.

Find the Balance of Connection and Detachment

Stay excited about what you do, experience it, but develop a sense of detachment from the vagaries or downside of the experiences.

JOURNEYING INWARD

During this time, we observe our strengths and weaknesses. We also go outside ourselves to assess our environments for opportunities and threats. In business this strategic planning is called SWOT analysis, an acronym for Strengths, Weaknesses, Opportunities, and Threats. In this section we discuss our inward journey to seek understanding. Here, we discuss your mission, values, defining moments, uniqueness, lifelines, strengths, weaknesses, symptoms, problems, and performance gaps.

DEFINE YOUR MISSION

In business, we talk about "mission" or reason for being. Why are you here? What do you want to be remembered for after your physical death? My mission includes adding beauty and good design in this world, and also relates to educating, sharing information and sharing love such as I am doing here.

Crystallize your Sense of Self so that you can proceed more effectively and efficiently into the future.

STUDY AND LIVE YOUR VALUES

We each have a set of values that we hold dear, and that underlies many of our decisions. Studying and clarifying your value system is helpful in coping with the "now" and in planning for the future. Identifying your values helps clarify the hoped-for outcomes of your decisions. Thus, decision-making has a guiding system that underlies it.

Try identifying four to six values that are underpinnings to your presence in this world. For example, my list includes: Humor, lifelong learning, integrity, beauty, freedom, and relationships.

IDENTIFY YOUR DEFINING MOMENTS

Defining Moments are those times of significant change where our true essence must rise to the surface, often for scrutiny by the rest of the world. What have been your Defining Moments? What makes you the person you are today? What choices have you made in your life from which you knew there was no turning back? Defining Moments often crystallize and communicate our core values. Write them down.

IDENTIFY WHAT MAKES YOU SPECIAL

What makes you different, unique or special in this world? There are multiple reasons to evaluate Self in this light. It may help your self-esteem, it will clarify your Self to yourself, it will help you move to the future with clearer understanding, and it will help you select the best options for your future.

FIND YOUR LIFELINES: ASSESS YOUR STABILITIES

If your boat is rocking, it is good to find your lifelines and your stabilities. Many very successful actors, actresses, athletes, or others in the limelight maintain homes where they grew up or where they feel a connection. It is how they stay grounded. What are your lifelines?

Find your connections, assess them for their future value (some may need to be left behind, if they are destructive), and repair and re-tie those lifelines. These lifelines may be relationships with God, with other people, with places, or with our treasured possessions. I encourage you to find the meaning in those relationships, to treasure them and to nurture them. If the boat seems like it is rocking a bit too much, imagine you are tethered to a lifeline that extends from your waist all the way to the center of the earth. This is a helpful exercise.

IDENTIFY YOUR STRENGTHS

Identify your strengths. Write them down and refer back to them. Find ways to leverage (use) them now and in the future.

IDENTIFY YOUR WEAKNESSES

Identify your weaknesses; write them down and begin dealing with them. Refer back to them, and add and delete as needed. Find ways to limit their impact, and to correct them if needed. Consider both the Now and the Future.

DISTINGUISH BETWEEN SYMPTOMS AND PROBLEMS

This takes some practice. Whenever you see as a problem, ask if this is really the problem or if it is a symptom of some other problem. If I am not exercising, for example, I see it as the problem until I am forced to analyze *why* I am not exercising. This may reveal that I am too busy, or that I am depressed, or that I am not feeling good about myself, or that I am procrastinating on taking the initiative to join a gym. If that is the case, I am usually procrastinating on other things as well.

ASSESS YOUR PERFORMANCE GAPS

Draw a circle. Divide it into the important components of your life, just as you would cut a pie. Examples might be: Financial, spiritual, relationships, physicality, surroundings, etc. Imagine the outer edge of the circle is a "10" (best) on every piece of that pie. Analyze where you are on each of the pieces of your life, using a scale from 1 to 10. Draw a line in each pie slice that depicts where you are now. This is your "performance gap" - the difference between where you are and where you want to be. Identify actions that will help correct each deficiency.

CONTINUE VISUALIZING

Visualizing the future is extremely important as we move through the process of creating and acting on goals. Draw the way you would like your life to look in, say, five years, or create a collage of magazine photos that represent concepts or possessions that you would like in your life in five years' time.

FIND YOUR LIFELINES

The great coyote watches the moon rise for the 2, 878, 697, 061, 812, 782 nd time.

ASSESSING YOUR BALANCE SHEET

Assessing your personal balance sheet is an important exercise to help launch forward movement. Here you assess your assets, asset-usage, assortment "potency," "debt," and consequences of actions.

ASSESS YOUR ASSETS

List your assets, both tangible (e.g., material possessions) and intangible (e.g., time). Identify your resources, be it money or a network of friends. Decide what you can do without, if necessary.

What can we do to make use of our strengths for our futures? Also, what do we do well that we can use to make others' lives better or to enhance this world we live in? Sharing ourselves can be revitalizing, even when it is off-goal. Utilize your assets!

ASSESS YOUR "ASSORTMENT POTENCY"

Stores have assortments of goods and people have assortments of assets. How potent is your assortment? Will it be helpful to you to trade off one thing for another, to increase the potency of your assortment?

For example, will selling some of your possessions give you more capital, which in turn will make you more potent in being able to act on opportunities that may arise? Do you have plenty of time, in which case you might want to further your education? Assortment potency is a useful concept!

Assess and Minimize your "Debt"

By "debt," I mean anything that may work against us and which creates a negative entry on your personal balance sheet. Physical debt includes not taking care of our bodies. Social debt includes outstanding grudges and the like. Personal debt includes self-loathing, for example, or even narcissism. What items in your life need correcting?

The idea of "debt" is that we are in a negative position that we will first have to pay or write off before we can take advantage of a desirable opportunity that comes our way. It puts us behind now and in the future. Try to rid yourself of debt now, before that opportunity becomes a missed opportunity. If you are looking to date, create in yourself the person you would like to be with by paying down those debts—lose the weight, quit smoking, mend broken fences, and pay the off the credit cards.

Manage Consequences to Others

"Systems theory" says that every move we make impacts others. We live in a universe — a system. When we make our shifts or respond to changes, we will impact everyone near us, and there will be a ripple effect to others even farther from us; i.e., when my mate and I separated, it impacted our friends.

Our decisions are not made in vacuums. We have the opportunity to create negative or positive consequences from our decisions. It is best to maximize the positives and minimize the costs of our actions to others. If I have a job offer in New York and another in California, and they are both equivalent, I will choose the job in California to be near my family. It is good for me, but it is also good for them. If I have a choice between painting my house a color others will enjoy, versus a color others will detest (assuming I like both colors), I will select the color that enhances others' lives rather than detracting from their life experience.

I do not mean that one should be self-sacrificing or be a martyr. I mean simply that we should acknowledge the effects of our actions, and try to reduce negative impacts, and increase positive impacts, when possible.

Balancing the Journey

So, here we are. We are working hard to understand our Self. We are working hard to cope. We are working hard to plan a future. It is easy to get stressed in all this working! Below are some little reminders and helpful hints that will aid in our continued journey of discovery and reinvention: being kind to your Self, respecting each day, enjoying the change of scenery, smelling the roses, seeking and appreciating the magic, and sharing good fortunes.

Be Kind to Your Self

Staying healthy is very important. Stress can ruin your health. If you are working too hard, or just not sleeping due to over-thinking, attend to it. I have seen many people lose their health due to stress-related illness. Health includes not just physical health, but mental, spiritual, financial, and professional well-being, as well.

RESPECT EACH DAY

Every day brings a new sunrise and a new opportunity to greet the world. I try to accomplish something everyday - even if it is pampering myself or feeling sorry for myself! Seriously, it seems useful to focus on the moment. If it is a bad moment, hold the feeling, experience it, and let it dissolve or fly away. Experience it, release it and move forward.

RESPECT EACH DAY

It was at the end of the longest day of the year and the gentle gunderswatch stood ever so quietly as they watched the sky slowly turn to night.

ENJOY THE CHANGE OF SCENERY

Whether it is success, loss or LifeShifts, take some time to enjoy and savor the process, and to be thankful for the change of scenery. Even if the change is something very dark in your life, finding its truth, its lesson or its silver lining can create an enlightening vantage point. Sometimes it takes time to achieve this, but it *is* a worthy goal.

Also, some suggest that we not make too many changes at one time. A slow start may be a wise, accelerating as you like the process and see results.

One never knows what is around the next turn. It might be something wonderful, especially if we have laid the groundwork to act on opportunities that may present themselves. Enjoy the change of scenery.

SMELL THE ROSES

Regardless of where you are in the process of life, it is important to know when to "stop and smell the roses" (yet another metaphor). It is so easy to get caught up in action that we forget our down-time, family time or time for inspiration or stimulation. It is often these "stop and enjoy" times that lead to renewed creativity or peace.

SMELL THE ROSES

Two coyotes lost in the moment, as ROMANCE returns to the Land of the Rock-Balancing Mts.

SEEK AND APPRECIATE THE MAGIC

A few years ago, I stopped in the parking lot of a restaurant at Big Sur, California, to switch drivers. The restaurant patio overlooked the ocean, but we did not walk out to it. As we took our new positions in the car, a maintenance worker called to us: "Aren't you going to look at the ocean? If you don't, you will miss the magic!" Here was a man who swept patios for a living, yet knew so very much about life.

We never know who will teach us something, so it is best to stay open.

SHARE

Don't forget to share your resources, whether it be offering a shoulder to someone in need, or taking cookies to the volunteer firemen. Love one another.

And don't be smug if your change is a positive one, such as winning the lottery!

Share

EARLY MORNING POKER GAME

Coyote always offers the losers a "Coyote is King" deck
of cards, personally signed by him. SG '83

LOOKING OUTWARD

Now that we have found some balance, we will continue our journey of coping, collecting information, and planning for tomorrow. Here, we discuss identifying your opportunities, threats, inflection points, undertow problems, and strategic gaps.

SCAN YOUR ENVIRONMENT

Earlier, I spoke of listening to your environment. Now, actively search your various environments for clues about future opportunities, threats, inflection points, undertow problems, or strategic gaps. These are covered in various places throughout this book.

IDENTIFY OPPORTUNITIES

Identify current and anticipate future opportunities. Write them down. Refer back to them. The goal is to maximize our ability to respond to opportunities, to have the resources ready when they are needed, and to be able to reach through an open window of opportunity and latch onto that opportunity to make it our own.

IDENTIFY THREATS

Assess (Now) and anticipate (Future) threats. Your goal is to minimize the impact of threats now and in the future. Write them down, reflect on them and take actions to avoid them. Imagine you are crawling across a field full of landmines. While still focusing on the goal of crossing the field, try to avoid these land mines.

Also, change your lenses, and look for opportunities among the threats. Remember,
. . . a problem is often just an opportunity in disguise. . .
Turn lemons into lemonade.

LOOK FOR INFLECTION POINTS

Inflection points are points of significant changes in one's environment. Identify those points from your past. They may have also been Defining Moments. Anticipate inflection points in the future. For example, we now talk about "post-9/11" - after the Trade Center bombing. That was a cultural inflection point, after which much else changed. Or, imagine that you are a maker of slide rules and that computer technology is being developed. Bang! It's on the market. You go to work. What will you do that day?

LOOK FOR UNDERTOW PROBLEMS

Undertow problems are less visible than inflection points. They are situations that, if unattended, may sweep you away just as an undertow current in the water might do. It might be a personal issue - an escalating dependence on drugs or alcohol, for example—or it might be operating in your surroundings.

When looking at the environment around you, and predicting what might happen in each, seek to unveil both inflection points and undertow problems.

IDENTIFY STRATEGIC GAPS

Strategic gaps are differences between where we want to be in the future, and where we *will* be, using our current strategies and actions. It is a concept that is looking to the future. If I am not saving money now, how will I have the retirement I need for my future? Look for the strategic gaps - project yourself into the future on the primary pieces of your life. What needs to change to make your future be what you want it to be, in each of the pieces that make up your life?

LOOK FOR UNDERTOW PROBLEMS

DRAMA AT THE BASE OF ROCK-BALANCING MTS. #2 + #3 (WITH SPOTS)

Coyote was so intent on searching out the Eternally Elusive milkbones that she jumped smack into the Gunderswatch. SG/85

TRYING ON "TOMORROW"

Change is scary. Sometimes we must slowly move from today's reality to tomorrow. As with products, sometimes "trial" is a great idea. Not always possible, but if we can try something on, it reduces our risks when we make the actual decision to adopt a new behavior, a new job or a new life.

LEARN FROM EXPERIENCES

Analyzing experiences and finding their "nuggets," or the meat of their nuts, brings richness to our futures, as well as wisdom. Some people say "Life is too short for being . . ." (unhappy, for example). A friend says "Life is too long for being . . . " (unhappy). Note where you thrive and where you wither. Write them down and attend to that information.

TRY NEW BEHAVIORS OR MINGLE WITH NEW PEOPLE

If our old behaviors are no longer effective, perhaps it is time to try new behaviors. Perhaps you have been playing the victim or perhaps you have been on a power trip which has turned people off. Try a fresh approach if your current actions are not successful. Take a class, temporarily color your hair, or work at an internship in an area in which you are weak.

Meeting new people and talking about new topics can change our perspective and give us alternative viewpoints. Joining a club of others with similar interests can feel great and networking can be fun!

Mingle With a New Crowd

Hot-Air Coyote finds himself in with a fast crowd.

MOVING FORWARD— CREATIVELY

We are grounded and have a grip on things, and are now ready to move forward. Here are some techniques for moving forward creatively. These include breaking up the task, getting prepared, using metaphors and acronyms, using action and positive energy, communicating effectively, and staying grounded and stable while doing so.

BREAK THE TASK INTO BITE-SIZED PIECES

If the big picture of what you need to do from here on is too overwhelming, break larger tasks into bite-sized pieces. This moves you from "overwhelm" to "action," and gives a sense of moving forward. Don't bite off more than you can chew!

One technique (Management by Objectives or MBO) has you list an objective at the top of a page, list in order all the component activities that will accomplish this objective, and record the date you perform each task. Rewrite the plan weekly, narrowing down each set of activities by performing them, and then ultimately accomplishing your goal. Similarly, use a bulletin board and file cards, pinning cards for major goals across the top. Then record tasks to complete each goal - one task per card- and arrange them sequentially in columns under each goal. Remove cards as tasks are completed. The columns shorten over time as you move toward goal achievement.

Don't worry about the touchdown—just the first down; then the next first down. Pretty soon you have a touchdown!

Don't Bite Off More than You Can Chew

SAILBOAT TAKEN BY A RATHER LARGE TROUT

Of course it was spat out immediately because of unsavory halyards and porcupine quills...

BE PREPARED; STAY PREPARED

This is a popular motto. Part of thinking ahead is to plan for opportunities, and to prepare your Self for their possible arrival. Education is an act toward the future, as is investing in one's spirituality, physical well-being or anything else that may help you better pounce on an opportunity that presents itself. It is so distressing to be caught unprepared!

Proactively prepare yourself for the opportunities you want to be able to act on. If it is a particular job you would like to be qualified for, create the skills you will need. If it is a particular person you want to be with, prepare yourself to be the person who will fit their needs.

I am not saying you should lose sight of your Self. What I *am* saying is that if you want to trek the Himalayas, you should start working out now. If you want to be in a relationship with a non-smoker, you should quit smoking now. If you want a career ladder, you should invest in education now.

Luck may just be opportunity meeting preparedness.

Be Prepared

READY FOR ANYTHING, RAINY OR SUNNY, TASTY OR BLAND

Caught in-between seasons, wondering what happened to spring

THINK METAPHORICALLY

A metaphor is a transfer of meaning from one thing to another. I once said that my life felt like I was a bug on a leaf in whitewater rapids. Thinking metaphorically has helped me through many situations. I can make those situations conform to whatever way is helpful to me, profound or funny. It also gives me some detachment, so that I don't get washed over by the wave. And, it seems to help with understanding situations.

I think of my life changes as the change in a riverbed. Will the change be permanent? What do I need to do to get the river back on course? If the river is going to stay with its new course, what opportunities are on its riverbank - things that were not on the old bank? While it is changing, it is often fairly mucky and yucky and muddy and all those messy things, just as my life felt on occasion. What were the metaphorical hip-waders in my life - the things that made walking through the mud of life more comfortable or palatable? Incidentally, metaphor is often also used in creativity exercises.

THINK OF ACRONYMS

I love creating acronyms that humor me, guide me, remind me, or give me a different perspective. The latest at my house is "OGRE: The Over-thinker's Guide to Rethinking Everything!" OGRE reminds me not to get caught up in over-thinking, but rather to be decisive and *act*.

THINK METAPHORICALLY

Bridge over Troubled Highway

KEEP MOVING

I have heard from many people about the importance of motion. Motion creates energy. If depressed, physical activity helps greatly by creating a positive chemical change in your body. For instance, at parties, aren't we attracted to the social butterflies more than to the wallflowers? More metaphors!

The same holds true in business. We stay away from restaurants that have no customers; we invest in stocks of businesses that show action; we like to mingle with those we perceive as "winners," or at least who appear to be interesting. If you are feeling stagnant professionally, or you have undergone change, you will be a more interesting job candidate if you are engaged in activities and show vitality. A gas station owner told me that when business was slow, he would service his own car at his station's island. His activity attracted notice and then customers.

SURROUND YOUR SELF WITH POSITIVE ENERGY

It is uplifting to surround yourself with positive people and positive feelings or with beauty or with anything else that gives you positive vibrations. Similarly, it can be very destructive to surround yourself with negative people, with negative attitudes or with negative surroundings. Our surroundings influence our moods, our actions, our decisions, and our options.

Keep Moving

Sometimes they just rushed around all day. SG.

TALK POSITIVELY

Positive talk will reinforce positive actions. Deleting negative words from your vocabulary can change your reality because it changes the way you describe your situation to your Self and to others. If you think, talk and act in a positive manner, you will "walk tall," as my mother would say.

CHANGE YOUR SURROUNDINGS

One tactic for enhancing creativity is to alter your surroundings. This is one reason that we take trips when we are feeling a bit confused. You can also alter your home or social atmosphere, or your memberships and clubs. New surroundings lead to new perspectives.

TURN THOUGHT TO ACTION

It is so easy to become complacent or dormant. Change often requires a time to care for one's Self, to renew one's spirit, to reanalyze one's situation. Such reflection can be good. But when do we stop thinking, planning and reacting, and become more action-oriented?

It takes action to get from here to there, just like we must walk, drive or *do something* if we are here and want to be there.

KNOW WHEN TO ACT

There are times to be quiet and times to act. Bold moves have a special magic and power. Pick your battles carefully.

KNOW WHEN TO ACT

Brand Yourself: Communicate Your Values

As you go forward, remember your values, live them and communicate them, personally and professionally. Just as we each have a name, we each have a "position" in others' minds. Create the positioning that is your truth so that you attract similar energy.

Watch Where You Step and Don't Wear Blinders

If things are going well, we may be whisked away by the excitement. If things are going poorly, we may become mired in our own problems, and forget to look where we are walking. It is true that we should "keep our eyes on the ball," rather than looking up when we are swinging the golf club.

On the other hand, there is an adage about "marketing myopia" - the railroads failed because they thought they were in the railroad business rather than in the transportation business. It is best to not wear blinders, but also good to know when to keep your eye on the ball.

Keep an Even Keel

It is so easy to get caught up in the whirlwind of careers going well, or our thriving personal situations. Fly high but stay grounded so that if the bubble pops, we do not fall too hard or too far. Appreciate the good times and stay grounded about the bad times. Remember that "this, too, shall pass." Life is not always smooth sailing. There are times we are running with the wind and there are times we are running into the wind, just as in sailing. Find the right breeze and fill the sails with air whenever possible. Tack, or change course when necessary!

Identifying Your Options

There are strategic planning tools for understanding options. Here I have rephrased them and reworked them so they are understandable, and so they apply to us as individuals. Feel free to make notes on thoughts, options and intentions.

Do What You Do, but Do It Better

One strategy available to businesses is called Market Penetration. It means serving current markets with current products, but doing it better than you did before, and doing it better than your competitors. The same option applies to individuals. Find what works and exploit it. Improve performance, consistently ratcheting up your standards. Always do your best.

Nurture a Niche

A "niche strategy" is serving one small market in a very deep and meaningful way. It may mean serving as many needs of your family as is humanly possible or doing every task you are able to for your employer or for a market.

DEVELOP NEW SKILLS

Another strategy for the future is to develop new skills to serve your current market (also called a product development strategy). As an individual, this might include adding a dimension to your home life that was not present before, adding a new role to your current committee or club functions, or adding a new skill for performing the job you currently have.

DEVELOP NEW MARKETS

This strategic option includes using your same skill base or personal characteristics to serve a different person, a different relationship or a different job. It is called a market development strategy. You stay the same, but who you serve or connect with changes.

DEVELOP NEW SKILLS

BEHAVIOR MODIFICATION

Coyotes learn to relate to sheep in a different way.

TEAM UP

Sometimes it is helpful to team up. This might mean getting married, finding a colleague to work with, hiring an assistant, hiring a life or business coach, going to a psychiatrist, or finding a friend to be a sounding board.

Teaming up takes many shapes and forms. It is an option that may help you cope or help propel you to your desired space in life.

Team Up

FIVE COYOTES TAKE THE TIME TO FIGURE IT ALL OUT.

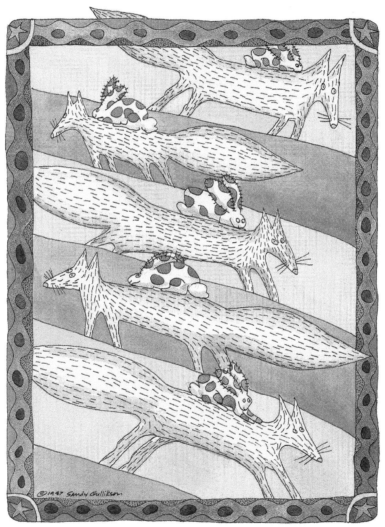

They'll either get to the bottom of it or be on top of it
ONCE AND FOR ALL!   S. Gullikson 1987

REINVENT YOURSELF

An option we all have is to reinvent ourselves. This might be a short-term fix or a more long-term plan, such as that which is required by transition and transformation.

Actions might be more superficial, such as changing our attire or image, or may be more internal, such as saying, "I want to become a nicer person." Businesses do this when the market for what they are currently offering begins to dry up.

INNOVATE

Innovation means to do something new or to be creative. Some of the most successful people and businesses have been successful because they were creative and insightful.

Strategic innovation means watching your environments and your Self, and creatively anticipating where you can put your skills and your Self to make the most impact in the future.

Reinvent Your Self

Coyote admiring his new cowboy boots   Sandy Gullikson © 1983

DIFFERENTIATE YOURSELF

Know what makes you different, unique and special. Communicate it effectively and create an image in others' minds. What does your employer value about you? What do your friends value? What do *you* value about yourself? Create the identity for which you want to be known. Be proud of your uniqueness.

MARKET YOUR SELF

Not only are you trying to ratchet up your performance, but you are also trying to ratchet up communication about what you have to offer. Be happy. Create positive energy. Sell your Self!!

Market Your Self

THE COYOTETTES & THE ARMADILLO BAND

The Coyotettes strut their stuff to the snappy melodies of C.E. Rabbit and the Armadillo Band.

UNDERSTANDING DECISION-MAKING

You have weathered the storms and now you are planning for tomorrow. It is very important to understand the information you have gathered, as well as your own decision-making. Here, we discuss asking the right questions, testing our assumptions, knowing our goals, knowing our criteria, and knowing our decision rules.

ASK THE RIGHT QUESTIONS

Asking the right questions often divides the successful from the unsuccessful. Asking the right questions is a skill to be developed.

TEST UNDERLYING ASSUMPTIONS

There is a business technique called "assumption surfacing and testing." It means that we look at our decisions, find what assumptions they are based on and then test those assumptions for validity. Are you closing off options because of faulty assumptions?

KNOW YOUR GOALS

By now, hopefully you have some insight about your goals. If not, think about what you want your life to look like in one year, in five years, in twenty years. Visualize it, write about it, draw it, or do whatever helps to clarify your vision.

ASK THE RIGHT QUESTIONS

THE ETERNAL QUANDARY

Coyote will sort out everything for you, more or less

KNOW YOUR CRITERIA

When deciding on future actions, can you identify four or five criteria to guide you? For instance, when deciding where to move, I assessed the distance to my family, the weather, the proximity to consulting jobs, and where I felt socially comfortable.

UNDERSTAND YOUR "DECISION RULE"

Decision rules help us to make decisions - simple as that. We might have one criterion, such as "my mother's health - I will do anything I have to do for my mother." Or, we might have several criteria, such as those I mentioned above. Or, we might have a cutoff criteria - "I won't go anywhere where it snows," leaving open many areas in the Southwest and West as options.

What is your decision rule? Does analyzing that rule improve your understanding of your viable options?

Enjoying the Journey

I hope the above strategies and tactics help you:
- understand change
- survive change
- cope with change
- and optimize change

Managing change is much better than just being swept about by it. Proactively managing our situations may, regardless of whether we wanted this change or not, place us in a more positive space than we would have been in had our course not been altered.

Being positive and staying positive can be difficult. If one is fearful, it is helpful to feel the fear in one's body and to feel it dissolve, so decisions are coming from a place of strength rather than coming from fear or a place of weakness.

People respond to situations differently. The thoughts and techniques I presented in this book are a culmination of my own experiences, my reading, and my teaching of business strategy. The book is meant to be helpful and is not meant to be derisive to anyone who believes strongly in the power of prayer or who believes in preordained destiny. It is meant merely to add to your tool box of skills. In that regard, I hope I have been successful. The ride of life can be truly joyful.

Enjoy the magic carpet ride!!!

With determination, you will not just survive.
You will prevail!!!

—The Beginning—

With the rose-colored glasses, Coyote saw that the world was really made of LOVE afterall.

©S. Gulliksen

Printed in the United States
by Baker & Taylor Publisher Services